LET'S LOOK AT

D1296326

LET'S LOOK AT
BRAZIL

BY JOY FRISCH-SCHMOLL

CAPSTONE PRESS
a capstone imprint

Pebble Plus is published by Capstone Press,
1710 Roe Crest Drive, North Mankato, Minnesota 56003
www.mycapstone.com

Library of Congress Cataloging-in-Publication Data
Names: Frisch-Schmoll, Joy, author.
Title: Let's look at Brazil / by Joy Frisch-Schmoll.
Description: North Mankato, Minnesota : Capstone Press, 2019. | Series: Pebble plus. Let's look at
countries
Identifiers: LCCN 2018029935 (print) | LCCN 2018031713 (ebook) | ISBN 9781977103895 (eBook pdf)
| ISBN 9781977103802 (hardcover) | ISBN 9781977105592 (pbk.)
Subjects: LCSH: Brazil—Juvenile literature.
Classification: LCC F2508.5 (ebook) | LCC F2508.5 .F75 2019 (print) | DDC 981—dc23

LC record available at https://lccn.loc.gov/2018029935

Editorial Credits
Erika L. Shores, editor; Juliette Peters, designer; Jo Miller, media researcher;
Laura Manthe, production specialist

Photo Credits
Getty Images: Bambu Productions, 13, Otavio de Souza/Stringer, 15; Newscom: Sipa USA/ Gilson
Borba/NurPhoto, 14; Shutterstock: Aleksandar Todorovic, 1, Alf Ribeiro, Cover Middle, Bram Smits,
Cover Bottom, Cover Back, BrazilPhoto, 17, Bruno Ismael Silva Alves, 19, Erni, 9, Filipe Frazao, 11,
GlobeTurner, 22 (Inset), Gustavo Frazao, 7, Kleyton Kamogawa, 22-23, 24, marchello74, 21, nate, 4,
Nick Fox, 8, R.M. Nunes, 5, Skreidzeleu, 3, SNEHIT, Cover Top

Note to Parents and Teachers

The Let's Look at Countries set supports national curriculum standards for social studies related
to people, places, and culture. This book describes and illustrates Brazil. The images support early
readers in understanding the text. The repetition of words and phrases helps early readers learn
new words. This book also introduces early readers to subject-specific vocabulary words, which are
defined in the Glossary section. Early readers may need assistance to read some words and to use
the Table of Contents, Glossary, Read More, Internet Sites, Critical Thinking Questions, and Index
sections of the book.

Printed and bound in China.
970

TABLE OF CONTENTS

Where Is Brazil?

Brazil is the largest country in South America. It covers almost half the continent. It is a bit smaller than the United States. Brazil's capital city is Brasília.

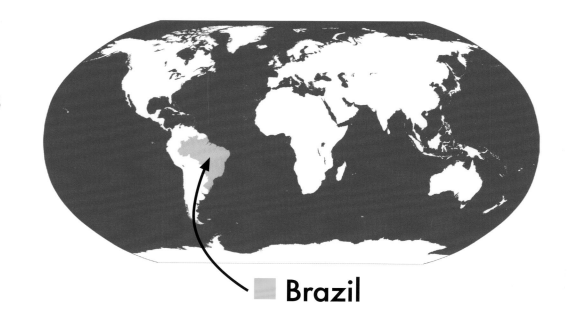

Brazil

Brasília, Brazil

From Rain Forests to Beaches

The Amazon River and the surrounding rain forest are in Brazil. Brazil also has hills, wetlands, and beaches. The weather is warm and wet all year.

The Wild Side

The rain forest is full of life.

Monkeys and parrots live

in the trees. Huge snakes called

anacondas live in rivers.

Wildcats hunt capybaras.

common squirrel monkeys

capybaras

People

The first Brazilians were Amerindians.
Starting in the 1500s, people came
from Portugal. Later, more people
came from Europe and Africa.
Most Brazilians live in large cities.

On the Job

Half of Brazilians help others through their jobs. These jobs include doctors, dentists, and teachers. Farmers grow sugarcane and coffee. Ranchers raise cattle.

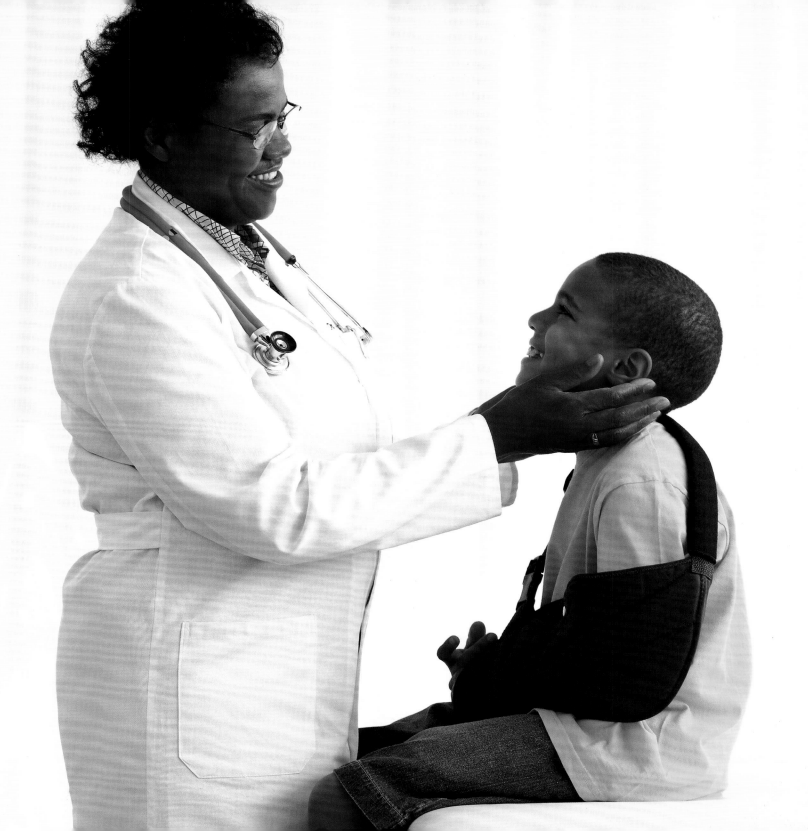

Carnival

Carnival is a festival in Brazil. It lasts one week. It happens just before Lent. People wear costumes and march in parades. Music and dancing fill the streets.

Kick! Score!

Soccer is Brazil's main sport.

Children play it on fields

and in streets.

The national team plays

in a large stadium.

Time to Eat

Brazilians eat a lot of rice and beans. One popular dish is feijoada. It has black beans and smoked meat.

Famous Site

A tall statue overlooks the city of Rio de Janeiro. It is called Christ the Redeemer. Its open arms welcome people to Brazil.

QUICK BRAZIL FACTS

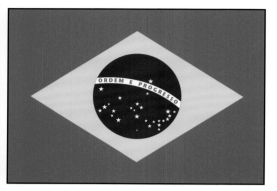

Brazil's flag

Name: Federative Republic of Brazil

Capital: Brasília

Other major cities: São Paulo, Rio de Janeiro, Salvador

Population: 207,353,391 (2017 estimate)

Size: 3,287,957 square miles (8,515,770 sq km)

Language: Portuguese

Money: Real

GLOSSARY

Amerindians—Indians native to South America

anaconda—a very large snake found in South America

capybara—a large, furry rodent that does not have a tail

continent—one of Earth's seven large land masses

Lent—the 40 days before the Christian holiday of Easter

rain forest—a thick forest of green plants that receives rain all year long

wetland—land that is low and wet, such as marshes or swamps

READ MORE

Klepeis, Alicia. *Brazil.* Exploring World Cultures. New York: Cavendish Square, 2017.

Orgullo, Marisa. *Celebrating Carnival!* New York: PowerKids Press, 2019.

Shields, Charles J. *Brazil.* Discovering South America. Philadelphia: Mason Crest, 2016.

INTERNET SITES

Use FactHound to find Internet sites related to this book.

Visit *www.facthound.com*

Just type 9781977103802 and go.

Super-cool stuff!

Check out projects, games and lots more at
www.capstonekids.com

CRITICAL THINKING QUESTIONS

1. Look at the photo of capybaras on page 9. Describe other animals you know of that are similar to capybaras.

2. Describe Carnival. What do you think it would be like to go to Carnival in Brazil?

3. Besides doctors and teachers, what are some jobs that help other people?

INDEX